Leaving My Homeland

A Refugee's Journey from Iran

Heather C. Hudak

CRABTREE
PUBLISHING COMPANY
WWW.CRABTREEBOOKS.COM

JAN 1 2 2018

CRABTREE
PUBLISHING COMPANY
WWW.CRABTREEBOOKS.COM

Author: Heather Hudak

Editors: Sarah Eason, Harriet McGregor, Wendy Scavuzzo, and Janine Deschenes

Proofreader and indexer: Wendy Scavuzzo

Editorial director: Kathy Middleton

Design: Paul Myerscough and Jessica Moon

Cover design: Paul Myerscough and Jessica Moon

Photo research: Rachel Blount

Production coordinator and Prepress technician: Ken Wright

Print coordinator: Katherine Berti

Consultants: Hawa Sabriye and HaEun Kim, Centre for Refugee Studies, York University

Produced for Crabtree Publishing Company by Calcium Creative

Publisher's Note: The story presented in this book is a fictional account based on extensive research of real-life accounts by refugees, with the aim of reflecting the true experience of refugee children and their families.

Photo Credits:
t=Top, bl=Bottom Left, br=Bottom Right

Inside: Flickr: Amnesty International/Richard Potts: p. 15b; Jessica Moon: p. 29b; Shutterstock: Sergei Bachlakov: pp. 22-23b; BalkansCat: p. 14; Best-Backgrounds: pp. 22-23; Brothers Good: p. 6t; ESB Professional: p. 29t; Grigvovan: p. 9b; Victor Jiang: p. 8b; Kipgodi: p. 26b; Lawkeeper: p. 11t; Loveshop: p. 5b; Macrovector: pp. 3, 4t, 17t; Martchan: p. 21t; Svetlana Maslova: p. 26t; MSSA: pp. 14tr, 15t, 28t, 29c; Matyas Rehak: pp. 5l, 7; Elena Rostunova: p. 19b; Saeediex: p. 16t; Olaf Schulz: p. 17b; Serkan Senturk: p. 11r; Tolga Sezgin: pp. 18-19c; Stoker-13: p. 16b; Vladmark: p. 9r; Weedezign: p. 24; Holla Wise: p. 13t; What's My Name: p. 18t; Daniella Zalcman: p. 6b; Zurijeta: p. 27l; Wikimedia Commons: José Cruz: p. 10; DIAC IMAGES: p. 21b; Mardetanha: p. 13b; Raminsahba: p. 8c; Hamed Saber: pp. 12-13c.

Cover: Jessica Moon; Shutterstock: Sebos.

Library and Archives Canada Cataloguing in Publication

Hudak, Heather C., 1975-, author
    A refugee's journey from Iran / Heather Hudak.

(Leaving my homeland)
Includes index.
Issued in print and electronic formats.
ISBN 978-0-7787-4687-4 (hardcover).--
ISBN 978-0-7787-4698-0 (softcover).--
ISBN 978-1-4271-2071-7 (HTML)

    1. Refugees--Iran--Juvenile literature. 2. Refugees--Australia--Juvenile literature. 3. Refugee children--Iran--Juvenile literature. 4. Refugee children--Australia--Juvenile literature. 5. Refugees--Social conditions--Juvenile literature. 6. Iran--Social conditions--Juvenile literature. I. Title.

HV640.5.I73H83 2018   j305.9'069140955   C2017-907648-5
    C2017-907649-3

Library of Congress Cataloging-in-Publication Data

Names: Hudak, Heather C., 1975- author.
Title: A refugee's journey from Iran / Heather Hudak.
Description: New York : Crabtree Publishing, [2018] |
  Series: Leaving my homeland | Includes index.
Identifiers: LCCN 2017054808 (print) | LCCN 2017057137 (ebook) |
  ISBN 9781427120717 (Electronic HTML) |
  ISBN 9780778746874 (reinforced library binding : alk. paper) |
  ISBN 9780778746980 (pbk. : alk. paper)
Subjects: LCSH: Refugee children--Iran--Juvenile literature. |
  Refugees--Iran--Juvenile literature. | Iran--Emigration and immigration-
  -Juvenile literature.
Classification: LCC HV640.5.I73 (ebook) | LCC HV640.5.I73 H83 2018
  (print) | DDC 305.9/069140955--dc23
LC record available at https://lccn.loc.gov/2017054808

Crabtree Publishing Company
www.crabtreebooks.com   1-800-387-7650

Printed in the U.S.A./022018/CG20171220

Published in Canada
Crabtree Publishing
616 Welland Ave.
St. Catharines, Ontario
L2M 5V6

Published in the United States
Crabtree Publishing
PMB 59051
350 Fifth Avenue, 59th Floor
New York, New York 10118

Published in the United Kingdom
Crabtree Publishing
Maritime House
Basin Road North, Hove
BN41 1WR

Published in Australia
Crabtree Publishing
3 Charles Street
Coburg North
VIC, 3058

What Is in This Book?

Leaving Iran

In Iran, the government wants to control people's beliefs and actions. It stops them from expressing opinions that are different from what the government believes. People in Iran cannot gather in groups to protest against things they disagree with. Those who do so are treated harshly.

People are also treated badly because of their religion, beliefs, or **ethnic group**. The government does not want its citizens to have beliefs or religions different from their own. There are also some **terrorist** groups in Iran. Because of this, many other countries will not do business with Iran.

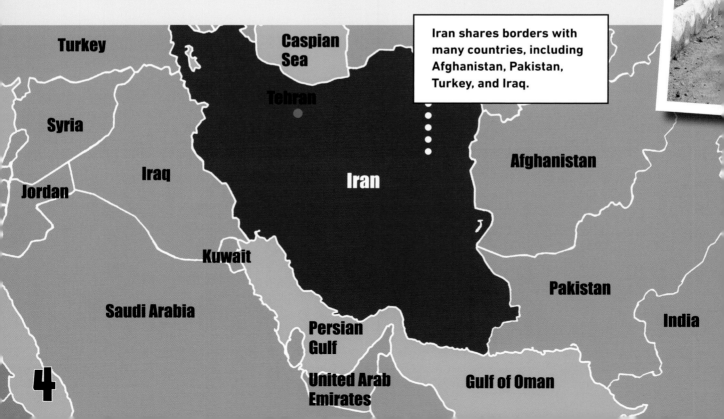

Iran shares borders with many countries, including Afghanistan, Pakistan, Turkey, and Iraq.

Turkey

Caspian Sea

Tehran

Syria

Afghanistan

Iraq

Iran

Jordan

Kuwait

Pakistan

Saudi Arabia

Persian Gulf

India

United Arab Emirates

Gulf of Oman

UN Rights of the Child

Every child has rights. Rights are privileges and freedoms that are protected by law. **Refugees** have the right to special protection and help. The **United Nations (UN)** Convention on the Rights of the Child is a document that lists the rights of children all over the world. Think about these rights as you read this book.

Iran's flag

Around 7 million Iranians do not have enough money to buy the basic things they need to survive, such as food and clothing.

Over the past several years, thousands of people have been killed or arrested by the government because of their different values. Many have left their homes to find safety. Some people remain in the country. They are called **internally displaced persons (IDPs)**.

Thousands of people have fled Iran. These people are refugees. Refugees flee their **homeland** because of unsafe conditions. They are different from **immigrants**. Immigrants choose to leave to look for better opportunities in another country.

My Homeland, Iran

Iran is a small country in Asia. It has mostly flat desert land that is surrounded by mountains. Nearly 83 million people live in Iran. Tehran is Iran's capital and its largest city.

Elburz Mountains
● Tehran

Zagros Mountains

Most people in Iran live near the Zagros Mountains in the west and the Elburz Mountains in the north.

More than 8 million people live in Tehran.

Before 1935, Iran was named Persia. Persian is the official language of Iran. Persians are the main ethnic group in the country. Other ethnic groups include Kurds, Balochs, Arabs, and Turkics. Most Persians are Muslim, which means that they practice the religion of **Islam**. There are two main branches of Islam: Sunni and Shia. Most Iranians are Shia Muslims.

This street is in Susa, Iran's oldest city.

Iran is one of the oldest countries in the world. People have lived there for tens of thousands of years. Iran's first big city, Susa, was built more than 5,000 years ago. The country has many beautiful buildings and gardens from long ago in history. Today, there are many modern buildings in Iran's cities, too.

Iran's Story in Numbers

More than

99 percent

of the people in Iran are Muslim. About

90 to 96 percent

are Shia Muslim, while

5 to 10 percent

are Sunni Muslim.

Zahra's Story: Life Before the Conflict

When I was little, I had a very good life in Iran. My family rented an apartment in a good neighborhood in Tehran.

Each morning, my mother woke up early and walked to the nearest bread store. She bought fresh, warm bread for breakfast. My favorite bread was a big, oval-shaped flatbread called noon-e tâftoon. Just the smell of it made my stomach growl. Some mornings, we had halim, a porridge made with mashed meat and wheat. We always drank chai shirin, a type of tea with sugar.

Flatbreads are a common food eaten by people all over Iran. Most Iranian families buy fresh bread each day.

All children in Iran must attend elementary school from ages 6 to 12.

My parents always believed education was important. My older brother and sister and I all went to a good school. We took extra classes a few times a week. School started at 7:30 a.m. each day. My favorite subject was math. I also took classes in art, sports, technology, and the **Quran**. Classes ended at 1 p.m. I played football with my friends after school.

Children play football in the street. Football, also known as soccer, is a very popular sport in Iran.

Lunch was the biggest meal of the day. My sister Anahita and I helped make it. We always had soup and salad to start. Then, we ate the main course. My favorite meal was grilled kebabs made of chicken or beef. My mother was a teacher. Each night, she helped us with our schoolwork. Then, we watched television or videos on YouTube before going to bed.

The Conflict in Iran

Iran has had **political** problems for many years. There was an uprising against the government between 1978 and 1979. Before then, Iran had one ruler, called the shah. The Shia Muslims who lived there did not like this, and forced the shah to flee.

A new government named the Islamic Republic took over. The people elected, or voted for, a new president. The new government made rules for Iran based on Islamic beliefs. Many people protested, and some left the country.

In 2005 and 2009, Mahmoud Ahmadinejad was elected president. Many people did not like him because of his strict beliefs.

Mahmoud Ahmadinejad was the president of Iran from 2005 to 2013.

UN Rights of the Child

You have the right to practice your own **culture**, language, and religion—or any you choose.

Ahmadinejad called for a harsh dress code, or way of dressing, and banned any music and television shows he thought did not fit with his beliefs. He treated some ethnic and religious groups, such as Sunni Muslims, very poorly. He did this because they had different ways of life or beliefs.

Many Iranians were unhappy. Millions of people protested. The government warned them to stop. When they did not, the government used force against them. Some protestors were beaten or killed.

Since 1979, laws in Iran have forced women to wear loose-fitting clothing to hide their body shape. They must also cover their hair.

Zahra's Story: Living Amid the Conflict

I was nine when Ahmadinejad was elected president for the second time. My family was very upset. The government did not always treat people fairly, especially Sunni Muslims. Even though my family was Shia, we wanted everyone to be treated equally. We wanted a new president to make things better. Other people felt the same way.

From our window, we could see protestors gathering after the election. My brother Ahmad went out to join them. But then the police arrived. They started beating people. I was so scared my brother would be caught.

Over the next few weeks, the government put a ban on the things we could do on the Internet. I was so mad that I could not watch YouTube anymore. Ahmad was mad, too. He said the government blocked websites so people could not speak poorly about it.

Following the election in 2009, 3 million people took to the streets of Tehran in protest.

Ahmad and his friends started going to protests all the time. At events, they sometimes even spoke about changing the way the government works. They had a **blog** where they shared their views about the government. A few of Ahmad's friends were arrested and taken to prison. My mother cried every time Ahmad left the house. She was worried the police would come for him, too.

Then, one day, a reporter asked to talk to Ahmad. The reporter wrote for a big newspaper. He wanted to help spread the word about what was happening in Iran. Ahmad agreed, even though he knew it would be dangerous for him.

The Iranian government controls what people can see on the Internet. They blocked many websites including Facebook and Twitter.

Nations Unite to Send Help

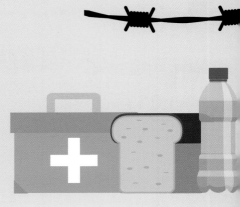

The UN is an organization that is made up of many countries. They work together to keep peace, and help people in need. The United Nations High Commissioner for Refugees (UNHCR) provides food, water, shelter, and health care to refugees. It also helps them find safe places to live.

Many Iranian refugees had to leave the country because they had different beliefs or ways of life than what the government supported. In Iran, people are not allowed be in a **same-sex relationship**. These people belong to the **LGBTQ** community. They are often treated poorly or even killed. This is because their way of life goes against the government's strict religious beliefs. Thousands have fled the country. The Iranian Railroad for **Queer** Refugees (IRQR) is a Canadian organization. It gives LGBTQ people money for food and shelter until they can find a safe place to live.

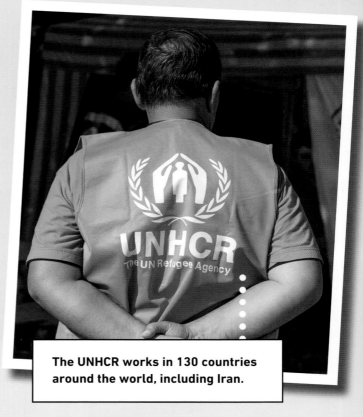

The UNHCR works in 130 countries around the world, including Iran.

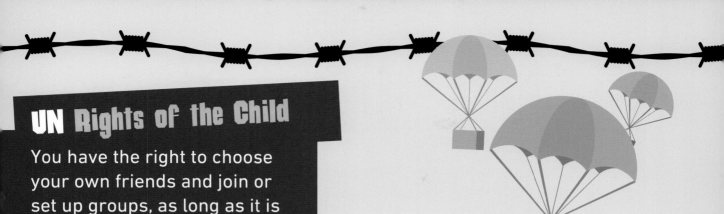

UN Rights of the Child

You have the right to choose your own friends and join or set up groups, as long as it is not harmful to others.

Amnesty International is an organization that helps countries fight for better **human rights**. In Iran, it is trying to stop the poor treatment of women and religious and ethnic groups. Amnesty International is trying to help Iranians gain the right to speak freely, hold protests, and gather as groups without being arrested or harmed.

Amnesty International exposes the way that the Iranian government treats its people.

Zahra's Story: Fleeing from Tehran

One night, the phone rang just as Anahita and I were getting ready for bed. No one ever calls that late. We knew it would be bad news. We pressed our ears against the door to listen. It was the police. They wanted to speak with Ahmad. The government had found out about his blog. They warned him to stop.

People in Iran are not allowed to openly express their opinions.

My father was angry with Ahmad. He had told him to stop the blog, but Ahmad did not listen. My mother was crying. She was worried the government would come after us. The newspaper story was coming out in a few days. I heard her say we must leave the country as soon as possible.

UN Rights of the Child

Your family has the responsibility to help you learn your rights, and to make sure that your rights are protected.

I was shaking and scared. I could not sleep. I loved my home. I did not want to leave my friends. The next morning, my father told us to pack a small bag with only a few clothes and one toy. I took my teddy bear. My mother's eyes were red and puffy from crying. So were Ahmad's.

*Neither of my parents went to work that day. Instead, they started to sell all of our things. They needed thousands of dollars to get us out of Iran. Finally, the day before the newspaper story came out, we got on a flight to Indonesia. From there, we would pay **smugglers** to take us to Australia.*

It takes more than 11 hours to fly from Iran to Indonesia.

17

What Paths Do Refugees Take?

Most people who leave Iran flee to Turkey. Today, there are about 30,000 **asylum** seekers from Iran living in Turkey. Most of the refugees live in cities. They must find jobs and homes of their own. Turkey does not have enough money or resources, such as food and shelter, to properly care for the refugees. A very small number of refugees live in camps built by groups such as the UNHCR.

Turkish refugee camps mainly house Syrian refugees, but there are some Iranians living there, too.

Iran shares borders with Iraq and Turkey. That is why refugees often enter or pass through those countries when they flee their homeland.

Turkey • • • • •
Tehran
Iraq
Iran

Iran's Story in Numbers

By 2011,

18,128

Iranians had applied for asylum in another country.

> **Most Iranian refugees live in cities and towns, and must rely on people they know to survive.**

Turkey does not allow Iranians to stay there forever. They must apply for refugee status with the UNHCR. They wait to be accepted into another country. This can take years. Iranians can live and work in Turkey until then. But it is often hard for them to find work. Those who do are often paid very little and are treated poorly. Language barriers make it hard to find jobs that pay well. Refugees may also face discrimination.

Thousands of Iranians have fled to Iraq. A small percentage of them live in camps. The rest of them must take care of themselves. Many do not feel safe. Often, the refugees cannot get enough food, water, and other items they need to survive. There is fighting between Iran and Iraq, too. Iranian refugees are sometimes the target of attacks by Iraqis and Iranian soldiers.

Zahra's Story: The Journey to Australia

We stayed in the big city of Jakarta in Indonesia for a few weeks. Then we got a call from the smuggler who would take us by boat to Australia. It was time for us to leave. We drove nearly three hours to get to the coast. I was so nervous.

When we got there, we had to wade out into the water to a small boat. We were soaking wet and shivering. The smuggler drove us out to a bigger boat. We were packed in like sardines with many other families like ours. We could barely move. The driver pulled a tarp over our heads. It was so dark. I could not see anything.

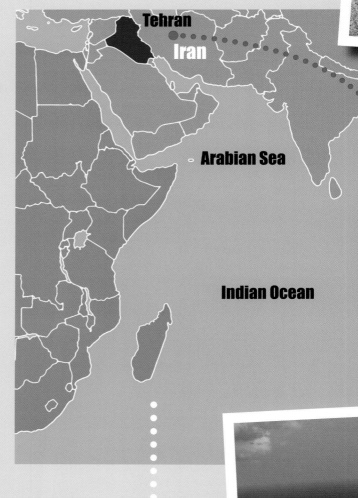

Tehran

Iran

Arabian Sea

Indian Ocean

Christmas Island is south of Indonesia in the Indian Ocean.

To get to a safe country, many refugees make a dangerous journey across rough waters. They travel in large, wooden fishing boats, like this one.

Indonesia

Jakarta

Christmas Island

Australia

Christmas Island is part of Australia. It has been used as an immigration detention center since 2001.

The ocean had rough waters with a lot of waves. The ride was terrible. It took only days, but felt like forever. A lot of people got sick. The smell was awful. The boats were old and not made for the rough waters. We had heard stories about them falling apart or tipping over. My mind was racing with fear. I barely slept at all.

We were lucky to arrive safely. It was late at night when we got to Christmas Island. The smuggler told us to stay in the boat overnight. We would have to go to a **detention center** for refugees in the morning. It poured with rain all night long. In the morning, some government workers took us to a building near a football field.

Iran's Story in Numbers

The journey across the Indian Ocean to Christmas Island is

200 miles

(322 km). It takes three days.

Some Countries Welcome Refugees

Iranian refugees may wait for many years before finding a permanent place to live. Countries such as Norway, Canada, the United Kingdom, and Australia take in Iranian refugees.

Some countries do not want Iranian refugees to live there. Many Iranians have fled their homes because they took part in protests against the government. These countries fear the refugees may cause problems in their countries, too. In some places, people wrongly believe that Iranians are terrorists because of their religion and the country's political unrest. Some people also think that Iranians might be violent because they are Muslim. This is called **Islamophobia**. It is unfair to label people like this. Refugees simply want a safe place to live. They are not terrorists.

United States: 600

This map shows where Iranian refugees applied for asylum in 2011.

In some countries, Muslims share their culture and religion at public events. This one is at Queen's Park in Toronto, Canada.

United Kingdom: 3,000

Sweden: 1,100

Denmark: 460

Iran

Australia: 2,150

Germany: 3,352

Netherlands: 929

UN Rights of the Child

Children have the right to a government that protects them. The government must help families protect children's rights, so that they can grow and reach their full potential.

Zahra's Story: My New Home in Brisbane

We did not stay on Christmas Island for very long. We were sent by plane to Manus Island in a new country called Papua New Guinea. We lived in a tent city there while we waited to get asylum in Australia. The conditions were not good there. We had little freedom. Some of the people we arrived with chose to go back to Iran. But we did not have a choice. If my brother went back, we were sure he would be sent to prison.

It can take years to be given a **host country**. Some people never get one. We were at Manus Island for about one year. Then the good news came. We were going to Brisbane, Australia. I was so excited.

Sometimes, refugee children who do not speak the local language can find it hard to fit in at school.

24

When we got to Australia, we were given some money to buy food and clothing. We got help finding a new home and a school. School is very different here. Boys and girls are in the same classroom. We went to separate schools in Iran.

My parents also got help finding jobs. My father got a job working with other refugees in a meat-processing plant. My mother works at night, stocking shelves at a department store. She misses teaching, so she helps teach refugee children.

Lots of people from other parts of the world live in Brisbane. We have been to special events where people from different cultures can get to know each other. We went to a drop-in center to make new friends and practice our English. My best friend is a girl named Amira. Her family fled from Iraq. We hang out every week and play games.

Iran's Story in Numbers

In total, there are about

35,000

Iranian people living in Australia.

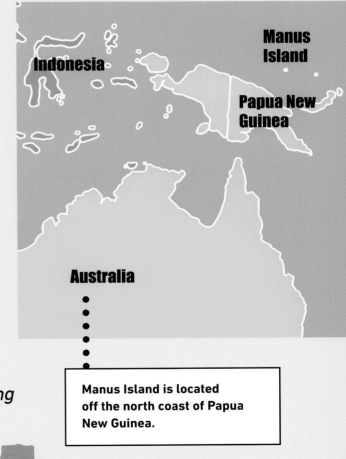

Indonesia

Manus Island

Papua New Guinea

Australia

Manus Island is located off the north coast of Papua New Guinea.

Challenges Refugees Face

Refugees often face many challenges in their new homes. The culture and ways of life in their host country can be very different from what they are used to.

Many refugees do not speak the same language as the people in their host country. That makes it hard to find a job, study in school, or make friends. It is not possible to fill out the forms that doctors, banks, and other services need. Even grocery shopping is a challenge for people who cannot read the food labels.

Refugees who do not know the language might find it difficult to travel around their new home. They cannot read street signs or bus routes.

UN Rights of the Child

You have the right to give your opinion, and for adults to listen and take it seriously.

In Iran, women must wear a hijab. This is a scarf that covers the head and neck. Their clothes must be loose-fitting and cover their arms and legs to their wrists and ankles. This is very different from the way people dress in some parts of the world. In Australia, women can wear any clothes they want.

Some countries are home to people from many cultures. They are free to say what they think and practice different religions. Refugees often come from places where that is not allowed. They may face discrimination if people view them as being "different."

Many refugees come from countries where it is common for many family members to live in the same house. They are used to helping one another.

You Can Help!

There are lots of things you can do to help make refugees feel welcome in your community. Reading books, looking at websites, and watching movies about different cultures is a good way to learn more about refugees.

☑ Donate to organizations that help refugees get settled in their host country.

☑ Volunteer to practice speaking English with a refugee.

☑ Have a party where everyone shares a part of their culture, such as food or clothing.

☑ Take newcomers on a tour of the community. Help them to find places such as stores and schools.

☑ Ask questions about the newcomers' cultures to get to know them better.

☑ Learn a few words in the newcomer's language, such as "hello" or "thank you." In Persian, to say "hello," you say "salâm" (sah-lohm).

Invite a refugee to spend time with you and your friends. This is just one way to help a refugee feel at home in a new country.

Discussion Prompts

1. What are the differences between an internally displaced person, a refugee, and an immigrant?
2. What challenges do refugees face in their host countries?
3. How can you help refugees feel at home in your community?

Glossary

asylum Protection given to refugees by a country

blog A website or page that is regularly updated

culture The shared beliefs, values, customs, traditions, arts, and ways of life of a group of people

detention center A place where people who have illegally entered a country are kept until the government decides where they should go

ethnic group Group of people who have the same background and culture

homeland The country where someone was born or grew up

host country A country that offers to give refugees a home

human rights Privileges and freedoms that all people should have

immigrants People who leave one country to live in another

internally displaced persons (IDPs) People who are forced from their homes during a conflict but remain in their country

Islam The religion and faith of the Muslim people

Islamophobia A fear or dislike of Muslims

LGBTQ Stands for lesbian, gay, bisexual, transgender, and queer. People in the LGBTQ community are often targeted because they have different ways of life from what many religions consider to be normal.

political Relating to the activities of the government and the people in power

queer People who are attracted to others of the same gender

Quran The religious text of Islam

refugees People who flee from their own country to another due to unsafe conditions

same-sex relationship A relationship between two men or between two women

smugglers People who move goods or people illegally

terrorist Someone who uses violence or intimidation to achieve political goals

United Nations (UN) An international organization that promotes peace between countries and helps refugees

Learning More

Books

Glynne, Andy. *Navid's Story: A Real-Life Account of His Journey from Iran.* Picture Window Books, 2017.

Leatherdale, Mary Beth. *Stormy Seas: Stories of Young Boat Refugees.* Annick Press, 2017.

Roberts, Ceri. *Refugees and Migrants* (Children of the World). Barron's Educational Series, 2017.

Websites

www.atozkidsstuff.com/iran.html
Visit this website to learn more about Iran. Click on some of the links to find Iranian stories, music, and recipes.

http://kids.nationalgeographic.com/explore/countries/iran
Explore more of Iran's history at this website from National Geographic.

www.unicef.org/rightsite/files/uncrcchilldfriendlylanguage.pdf
Learn more about the United Nations Convention on the Rights of the Child.

Index

About the Author

Heather C. Hudak has written hundreds of books for children and edited thousands more. She loves learning about new topics, traveling the world, and spending time with her husband and many pets.